Business Minded

Get In Soul

This Journal Belongs To

_____

Dedicated To Every Current And Future Business Owner Who Is Not Afraid To Just Do It.

Table Of Contents

How To Use This Journal	7
About Me	8
About My Business	24
#BusinessGoals	27
Past Mistakes And Failures	30
Legalities	34
Funding	39
Investor/s	41
The Competition	46
Style Of Operation	50
Product(s)/Service(s)	52
Pricing	56
Marketing Research Strategies	61
About My Customers	65
Customer Cycle	74
Marketing/Advertising: Online/Offline	76
- Online	77
- Offline	88
The Game Plan - Branding	98
Web Design	105
Apps	112
Physical Location	116
Now Hiring	122
Running The Numbers	126

Table Of Contents

- Sales Forecast   134

- Expense Budget   136

- Income Projections For The Next Twelve Months   138

- Breakeven Analysis   140

My Business Inspirations   142

Business Minded Daily   144

How To Use This Journal

There are days when we wonder how in the world will we ever get our business/es off the ground. You have probably tested many ideas to get your business to the next level by doing your research on certain strategies and putting them into practice. The outcome is good on some days, but there are those days where you can feel as if you do not know where your business is going. You may even ask yourself if this business is still worth another try? Is it time to expand or is it time to cut back? Or maybe you are just getting started. You might of realized that you need to get organized and write out a clear vision for your business. All these questions and ideas playing in your mind can be sorted out in this journal. This journal is all about holding you accountable with consistent practices to grow you and your business/es. This is the place where goals, strategy and execution is all planned out.

Use this journal as your personal business planner. Remember, one of the ingredients to a successful business is a thought out, meticulous and organized plan. This journal is your accountability partner and may become your business's best friend. There are motivational quotes throughout this journal that you can cut out and put on a wall or anywhere that you look at daily to inspire you. These quotes are simple reminders to keep you motivated and focused to achieving your goals regardless of the consequences. We encourage you to trust the vision that has been given to you as we believe it is well worth the journey.

To effectively use this journal, it is recommended to fill out the first half of this journal in the morning right before you start working and the second half of this journal once your work day is over. Filling out your business journal daily keeps you accountable and on track. Over time you will start to notice how far you have come. This is your business blueprint and business planner all in one. You are the one with the vision which means you are the only one who can execute your exact vision if you choose to be focused, organized and teachable. Regardless if you are just starting your business out alone and have no clue as to how to start or if this is your second or third attempt with a business idea, we believe you will succeed as long as you are dedicated, open to learning, willing to get up when you fall and most importantly praying over your business. You were built for this. So, let's get started.

About Me

About Me

Current Age:

I Am:

I Am From:

I Have Always Dreamed:

I Believe I Can:

About Me

I See Myself:

I Have Always Been Great At:

My Strengths Are:

My Weaknesses Are:

How Do I View Success?

About Me

How Do I View Fear?

How Do I View Risk?

I Carry An Attitude Of:

The People I Keep Around Me:

My Mentors Are:

About Me

People I Look Up To:

My Personal Goals Are:

Actions I Take Daily Towards My Personal Goals:

The Reasons Why I Want Or Wanted To Start A Business:

What Kind Of Business Would I Like To Start Or Have Already Started?

About Me

I Am Thankful For:

My Intentions With My Business:

I Am Aware:

I Am Scared To:

I Am Insecure About:

About Me

I Am Tired Of:

I Look Forward To:

I Want To Change:

I Have Heard:

When I Feel Overwhelmed, I:

About Me

My Family Has Told Me:

My Friends Have Told Me:

I Am Ignoring:

I Am Happy That:

I Am Choosing:

About Me

I View Myself:

I Have Failed At:

I Have Learned:

I Am Learning:

I Will Not Give Up On:

About Me

I Am Motivated By:

God Has Revealed To Me:

Books I Have Read:

My Current Morning Routine:

My New Morning Routine I Plan To Establish:

About Me

How Do I Deal With Problems?

I Am Special Because:

I Currently Own:

What I Know About Myself:

What I Want Others To Know About Me:

About Me

I Want More:

I Deserve:

I Was Taught:

Currently I Am Struggling With:

I Started Doing:

About Me

I Stopped Doing:

I Am Making It A Priority To:

I Have Realized:

Nothing Will Stop Me From:

I Pray:

About Me

I Know I Can:

I Will Always Find A Way:

I Plan To Invest In Myself By:

I Am Doing This For (A List Of My What And Whys):

I Have A Mindset That:

About Me

I Believe My Purpose Is To:

Is This My First Business?

I Am Excited About:

I Am Nervous About:

My Business Affirmations:

About Me

I Am Pursuing My Dreams Because:

About My Business

About My Business

My Business Name:

My Business Website:

My Business Contact Information:

My Business Location/s:

My Business Niche:

About My Business

My Business Partner/s (List If Any):

My Business's Social Media Channels, Handles & Names:

#BusinessGoals

#BusinessGoals

My Business Goals:

My Goals With My Customers:

My One Month Goal From Today:

My Next Quarter Goal:

My Six Month Goal From Today:

#BusinessGoals

My One Year Goal From Today:

My Five Year Goal From Today:

My Ten Year Goal From Today:

What I Want To Attract For My Business:

My Business Goal Of Impact:

Past Mistakes And Failures

Past Mistakes And Failures

How Do I Handle Failures?

When I Make A Mistake, I:

When I Fail At Something, I:

Businesses And Partnerships That Have Not Worked Out In The Past (Answer If Applicable)?

Based On My Response To The Previous Prompt, Why?

Past Mistakes And Failures

What Have I Learned Since My Biggest Mistake Thus Far?

Mistakes I Have Made With Money:

Mistakes I Have Made With Customers (Answer If Applicable):

Mistakes I Have Made Due To Lack Of Knowledge:

Mistakes I Have Made Because Of Ego:

Past Mistakes And Failures

Mistakes I Have Made From Not Having A Mentor:

Mistakes I Have Made From Listening To The Wrong Person/People:

Legalities

Legalities

How Will I Structure My Business?

Where Will My Business Be Structured?

Will My Business Need Insurance?

Have I Set Up A Business Checking Account?

Have I Set Up A Business Savings Account?

Legalities

How Will I File My Taxes?

How Often Will I Pay Sales Tax?

Where Will I Register My Business?

Will I Need To Trademark My Business Name And/Or Products?

Will I Need A Patent (If Yes, Write Down To What)?

Legalities

Will I Need To Copyright Anything (If Yes, Write Down To What)?

Does My Business Need An EIN/Business Identification Number?

Does My Business Need Any Permits And/Or Licenses?

Do I Have/Need Employment Agreements?

Do I Have An Online Terms Of Use?

Legalities

Do I Need Non-Disclosure Agreements?

If Yes To The Previous Prompt, Do I Have A Non-Disclosure Agreement?

Do I Need An Online Privacy Policy?

Do I Have Paperwork For Potential Investors?

Do I Have A Reliable Attorney To Take Care Of All My Legal Business Structure Needs?

Funding

Funding

How Will I Fund My Business?

How Much Money Do I Need To Fund My Business?

How Much Money Do I Need Every Month To Run My Business?

I Can Get Funds From:

How Do I Plan To Pay Back Any Funds Loaned To Me (Answer If Applicable)?

Investor/s

Investor/s

Will I Need An Investor(s)?

Will I Have Investors?

How Do I Know I Need An Investor/s?

What Would I Use The Funds From An Investor For?

What Should I Look For In An Investor?

Investor/s

What Does My Ideal Investor Look Like?

What Does My Investor/s Do?

How Often Would I Seek An Investor?

Would I Like An Active Or Silent Investor?

How Many Investors Would I Need/Want?

Investor/s

What Are The Different Types Of Investors That Would Be Good For My Business?

What Am I Willing To Give Up To Get An Investor?

What Will Investors Need From Me?

What Will I Need To Provide To Potential Investors For Funding?

How Would I Plan To Pay My Investor(s) Back?

Investor/s

How Would I Attract Investors?

The Competition

The Competition

Who Are My Direct Competitors?

Who Are My Indirect Competitors?

How Do My Competitors Position Themselves?

What Makes My Competitors Unique?

How Do My Competitors Brand Themselves?

The Competition

Do My Competitors Appeal To A Particular Group Of People?

What Do I Know About My Competitors?

What Do I Need To Know About My Competitors?

What Are My Competitors' Strengths?

What Are My Competitors' Weaknesses?

The Competition

What Makes My Competitors My Competition?

What Is My Competition Doing That I Can Do Better?

What Is My Competition Doing That I Will Not Be Doing?

Style Of Operation

Style Of Operation

How Does My Business Currently Operate (Answer If Applicable)?

How Do I Want My Business To Operate?

How Will I Prepare For Growth?

How Will I Prepare For The Holiday Season?

Product(s)/Service(s)

Product(s)/Service(s)

What Will I Be Offering?

What Makes My Product(s)/Service(s) Unique?

Will My Product(s)/Service(s) Be Wanted/Needed Ten Years From Now?

What Other Companies/Businesses Offer What I Offer?

I View My Product(s)/Service(s):

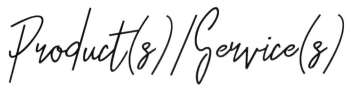

Product(s)/Service(s)

When Will My Product(s)/Service(s) Be Offered?

Where Will My Product(s)/Service(s) Be Offered?

Is There A Popular Season For My Product(s)/Service(s)?

Does My Product(s)/Service(s) Bring Back Repeated Customers?

Over Time How Do I Plan To Expand My Product(s)/Service(s)?

Product(s)/Service(s)

Why Am I Offering My Product(s)/Service(s)?

Who Would Benefit From My Product(s)/Service(s)?

My Product(s)/Service(s) Produces:

My Product(s)/Service(s) Has Helped Me/Others:

My Product(s)/Service(s) Will Be Packaged:

Pricing

Pricing

I Will Price My Product(s)/Service(s):

What Is My Pricing Determined By?

Who Determines My Price?

My Price Covers:

Is My Pricing Competitive?

Pricing

When People Purchase My Product(s)/Service(s), They Are Paying For?

What Is The Perceived Value Of My Product(s)/Service(s)?

What Is The Wholesale Price Of My Product(s)/Service(s) (Answer If Applicable)?

Other Companies Price The Same Product(s)/Service(s) For:

Will I Ever Raise My Prices?

Pricing

If The Answer To The Previous Prompt Is Yes, When?

How Much Value Do I Believe My Customers Are Receiving From My Product(s)/ Service(s)?

Will I Ever Offer Any Discounts?

If The Answer To The Previous Prompt Is Yes, When?

What Is A Comfortable Price For Me?

Pricing

What Is An Uncomfortable Price For Me?

How Much Would I Pay For My Own Product If I Was The Customer?

My Price Welcomes:

My Price Discourages:

Marketing Research Strategies

Marketing Research Strategies

What Are My Marketing Research Strategies?

What Will I Be Researching?

How Often Will I Research?

How Will I Gather Data?

Will I Hire Someone Else To Do My Research?

Marketing Research Strategies

The Research Will Help:

A Break Down Of My Marketing Research Strategy In Detail....

About My Customers

About My Customers

Is My Customer Male And/Or Female?

My Ideal Customer:

My Customers Like:

My Customers Age Ranges From:

My Customers Live:

About My Customers

My Customers Listen To:

My Customers Use:

My Customers Like To Be Spoken To:

My Customers Aspire To Be:

My Customers Consume Information (Write How):

About My Customers

How Do My Customers Find Out About New Products?

The Average Annual Salary Of My Customers:

The Highest Level Of Education Of My Customers:

What Do My Customers Do To Bring In Income?

Do My Customers Own Or Rent Or Live With Parents/Roommates?

About My Customers

What Type(s) Of Personalities Do My Customers Possess?

What Motivates My Customers?

What Motivates My Customers To Buy?

Why Do My Customers Buy?

When Do My Customers Buy?

About My Customers

How Do My Customers Buy?

How Much Money Does My Ideal Customer Spend On Luxuries?

How Does My Ideal Customer Feel About Purchasing Luxuries?

What Are My Customers Pain Points?

What Are My Customers' Issues?

About My Customers

What Do My Customers Think About My Competition?

What Do My Customers Expect When Purchasing From A Business/Brand?

What Do My Customers Think About My Product(s)/Service(s)?

Do My Customers Value "Good" Over "Fast" Or Both?

Do My Customers Like Things Personalized?

About My Customers

What Are My Customers' Spending Habits?

Who Are My Customers' Influencers?

Where Can I Find My Customers?

What Do My Customers Spend A Lot Of Money On?

What Do I Want My Customers To Know?

About My Customers

What Do My Customers Want To Know?

What I Want My Customers To Feel Is:

How Do My Customers Want To Feel?

The Number One Reason Why My Customers Would Come Back To Me/My Business:

Customer Cycle

Customer Cycle

How Do I Get My Customers To Purchase?

How Do I Upsell To My Customers?

How Do I Downsell To My Customers?

How Do I Get My Customers To Purchase A Higher Ticket Item?

How Do I Get My Customers To Spread The Word About My Business?

Marketing/Advertising: Online/Offline

Marketing/Advertising:

Online

I Believe Online Marketing/Advertising:

How Will I Market/Advertise Online?

How Will I Use Internet Marketing/Advertising To Attract New Customers?

How Will I Engage With Customers Online?

Online

What Social Media Platforms Will Myself/Product/Service/Business/Brand Participate In?

How Will I Use Social Media?

How Will I Market/Advertise Myself/Product/Service/Business/Brand On Social Media?

Do I Plan To Be Active On Social Media By Commenting/Liking And Sharing Regularly?

Will I Work With Social Media Influencers?

Online

Will I Pay Social Media Influencers?

How Will I Create And Maintain A Powerful SEO (Search Engine Optimization) Presence?

Is SEO (Search Engine Optimization) Important To Myself/Product/Service/Business/Brand?

Will I Use Email To Market Myself/Product/Service/Business/Brand?

How Will I Collect Emails?

Online

How Will I Build An Email List?

What Do I Plan To Say In An Email?

How Many Times Do I Plan To Send Out Emails?

Will I Be Using Press Releases For Myself/Product/Service/Business/Brand?

Will I Be Blogging?

Online

Will I Create Videos For Myself/Product/Service/Business/Brand?

How Will I Collect Reviews And Social Proof?

Will I Host Webiners?

If Yes To The Previous Prompt, What Kind Of Webiners?

Will These Webinars Be Free?

Online

Will I Partner/Collaborate With Anyone For Myself/Product/Service/Business/Brand?

If Yes To The Previous Prompt, Who And Why?

What Do I Believe Is A Prerequisite For A Good Collaboration?

How Do I Plan To Generate Online Press?

Will I Join Industry Online Forums?

Online

How Do I Plan To Generate Online International Press?

Does Myself/Product/Service/Business/Brand Need Content Marketing Such As Writing Articles, Blog Posts Etc.?

How Long Would I Do Online Paid Marketing Vs. Free Online Press?

What Paid Online Marketing/Advertising Tactics Will I Focus On Right Now?

What Free Online Marketing/Advertising Tactics Will I Focus On Right Now?

Online

What Is My Daily Online Marketing/Advertising Budget?

What Is My Weekly Online Marketing/Advertising Budget?

What Is My Monthly Online Marketing/Advertising Budget?

What Is My Quarterly Online Marketing/Advertising Budget?

What Is My Annual Online Marketing/Advertising Budget?

Online

Will I Be Doing The Marketing/Advertising Myself?

If I Pay For An Online Marketing/Advertising Expert, What Should I Look For And Ask?

With Marketing/Advertising, It Is Important To Me That:

How Will I Learn To Market My Product(s)/Service(s)?

Who Is A Great Example To Me In Terms Of Marketing/Advertising Similar Product(s)/Service(s)?

Online

What Kind Of Information Will I Be Putting Out Through Online Marketing/Advertising?

How Will I Collect Information To See If Online Marketing/Advertising Works For Myself/Product/Service/Business/Brand?

My Online Marketing/Advertising Strategies In Detail....

Marketing/Advertising:

Offline

I Believe Offline Marketing/Advertising Is:

How Will I Market My Product(s)/Service(s) Offline?

How Will I Create An Offline Buzz?

In What Ways Will I Market Myself Offline And/Or My Product/Service/Business/ Brand Locally?

Offline

In What Ways Will I Market Myself Offline And/Or My Product/Service/Business/Brand Nationally?

In What Ways Will I Market Myself Offline And/Or My Product/Service/Business/Brand Internationally?

What Paid Offline Marketing/Advertising Tactics Will I Participate In?

What Free Offline Marketing/Advertising Tactics Will I Participate In?

Will I Participate In Offline Guerrilla Marketing/Advertising Tactics?

Offline

If Yes To The Previous Prompt, What Are Some Offline Guerrilla Marketing Tactics That I Plan To Participate In?

Will I Hire A Marketing Firm For Offline Marketing/Advertising?

If Yes To The Previous Prompt, What Questions Should I Ask A Marketing Firm To See If They Are Qualified To Represent My Business/Brand?

How Will I Talk To Local Customers Offline?

Will I Use Billboards To Promote Myself/Product/Service/Business/Brand?

Offline

If Yes To The Previous Prompt, What Will The Message Convey About Myself/Product/ Service/Business/Brand?

Will I Use Speaking Engagements To Promote Myself/Product/Service/Business/Brand?

If Yes To The Previous Prompt, What Message Will I Convey That Will Help Myself/ Product/Service/Business/Brand?

Will I Host Events?

If Yes To The Previous Prompt, What Kind Of Events Will I Host To Promote Myself/ Product/Service/Business/Brand?

Offline

Will I Mail Out Physical Letters/Flyers/Catalogs?

If Yes To The Previous Prompt, What Will The Message Convey About Myself/Product/Service/Business/Brand?

Do I Have Business Cards?

If Yes To The Previous Prompt, What Is On My Business Card?

Do I Have A Brochure?

Offline

If Yes To The Previous Prompt, What Is In My Brochure?

If I Responded No To The Prompt 'Do I Have A Brochure?' And Plan To Get One, What Will Be Within My Brochure?

Will I Need A Street Team?

If Yes To The Previous Prompt, What Will My Street Team Do?

What Is My Street Team's Purpose?

Offline

Will I Advertise Using Newspapers And Magazines?

Will I Join Community Events?

If Yes To The Previous Prompts, Which Ones?

How Much Of My Time Each Day Will I Invest To Offline Marketing/Advertising?

How Much Of My Monthly Budget Will Go Towards Offline Marketing/Advertising?

Offline

The Resources Needed To Market/Advertise Offline:

How Will I Collect Information To See If Offine Marketing/Advertising Works For My Business?

I Believe Television Advertising:

I Believe Radio Advertising:

I Believe Product Placement Is:

Offline

I Believe Advertising With Magazines Would Hurt/Help Myself/Product/Service/ Business/Brand By:

My Offline Marketing/Advertising Strategies In Detail....

The Game Plan - Branding

The Game Plan – Branding

What Is The Goal Of Business Branding?

Why Is Branding Important To Me?

How Will I Brand Myself?

How Will I Brand Myself/Product/Service/Business?

What Will My Branding Colors Be?

The Game Plan – Branding

What Will Be My Branding Voice?

What Position Does My Brand Take In My Market?

What Is My Business's Mission?

What Is My Business's Purpose?

How Will I Build My Tribe?

The Game Plan – Branding

How Will My Brand Be Seen On Social Media And Other Forms Of Media?

What Is My Product/Service/Business/Brand Message?

What Are My Branding Goals?

What Is My Logo?

What Is My Tagline?

The Game Plan – Branding

Do I Have Consistent Brand Templates?

How Will I Get Customers To Recognize My Product/Service/Business/Brand?

What Is My Brand Image?

What Is My Brand Font?

How Will I Roll Out Brand Changes In The Future?

The Game Plan – Branding

Key Qualities And Benefits That My Brand Offers?

What Is The Culture Of My Business/Brand?

What Is My Written Style Guide And What Does It Consist Of?

How Will My Brand Build Trust?

How Will I Increase Brand Awareness?

The Game Plan – Branding

How Will My Brand Build Credibility?

How Will My Brand Attract Customers?

Is My Brand Relatable?

How Much Time And Resources Will I Spend Towards Building My Brand?

Where Will My Brand Be Seen?

Web Design

Web Design

What Will My Website Url Name(s) Be?

What Are My Website Colors?

Important Information Needed On My Website:

My 'About Me' Section On The Website Covers:

What Will It Cost To Maintain My Website?

Web Design

How Will I Make My Website Mobile Friendly?

How Will I Make Sure My Website Loads Fast?

My Website Must Haves:

My Contact Information On The Website Will Be:

Who Will Be Managing My Website?

Web Design

Who Will Update My Website With New Content And Make Changes As Needed?

Who Will Be Answering Customer Service Questions From The Website?

What Will The Homepage Display?

How Often Will The Homepage Be Updated?

How Will I Convert People On The Website?

Web Design

How Will I Collect Information From Visitors On The Website?

What Information Will I Collect From Visitors On My Website?

How Will I Display My Product(s) And/Or Service(s)?

Will I Have A Shop/Booking System On My Website?

How Will I Set Up My Sales Funnels For My Product(s)/Service(s)?

Web Design

Will I Need/Have Subdomains?

Who Will I Host My Website With?

What Additional Costs Will My Website Occur?

How Will I Customize My Website SEO (Search Engine Optimization)?

What Keywords Are Important To My Website That Is Related To My Business?

Web Design

How Do I Deal With Broken Webpages/Websites?

How Will I Intergrate Social Media To My Website?

How Will I Get Visitors To Stay On My Site For Longer Than A Few Seconds?

What Will Be My CTA (Call To Action)?

Apps

Apps

Does My Business Need An App?

What Kind Of App Would I Want To Create?

What Is The Aim Of My Mobile App?

How Would An App Be Beneficial To My Business?

Who Would Benefit From My App?

Apps

What Makes My App Stand Apart From The Rest?

Will My App Support Offline Mode?

How Will Customers Know I Have An App?

Will My App Be Available To Everybody?

Where Will My App Be Available/Listed?

Apps

Who Will Maintain My App?

What Problem Does My App Solve?

What Operating Systems And Devices Will My App Function On?

What Is The Blueprint Of My App From Beginning To End Once My App Is Downloaded?

Physical Location

Physical Location

Where Is My Store/Office/Warehouse Located (Or Will Be Located)?

How Much Space Do I Have Or Need?

Am I Buying Or Leasing My Location?

How Much Is The Lease/Mortgage Every Month?

How Much Will/Does It Cost Me To Maintain My Physical Location Each Month?

Physical Location

Am I In A Plaza Or Stand Alone Location?

Do I Have Signage?

Where Will I Get Signage From If I Do Not Have Signage?

How Much Would A Build Out Cost Me?

What Does My Physical Location Need?

Physical Location

Who Will Be Working At My Physical Location?

What Will Be The Positions Of Those Working At My Physical Location?

What Does My Physical Location Offer?

What Are My Physical Location Hours?

Would I Be Located Close To Any Of My Competitors?

Physical Location

Grand Openings And Other Events I Plan To Host At My Location:

What Are My Store/Office/Warehouse Location Policies?

What Kind Of Insurance Is Needed For My Physical Location?

What POS (Point Of Sale) System(s) Will I Be Using At My Physical Location?

The Daily Duties Needed To Keep My Physical Location Organized:

Physical Location

What Kind Of Security System Will My Physical Location Need?

What Kind Of Business Supplies Will My Physical Location Need?

Now Hiring

Now Hiring

Who Do I Currently Have Working With Me?

Who Would I Like To Work With?

What Positions Will I Be Hiring For?

What Will Be The Benefits Offered To Anyone Working With Me?

What Kind Of Employees Will I Be Working With?

Now Hiring

Who Do I Plan On Hiring Within The Next Month?

Who Do I Plan On Hiring Within The Next Quarter?

Who Do I Plan On Hiring Within The Next Year?

Who Will I Hire To Work Full Time In House?

What Do I Plan To Outsource?

Now Hiring

How Often Will I Pay The People I Hire?

How Long Will I Need Some Of These Positions?

Where Will The People I Hire Be Working From?

Running The Numbers

Running The Numbers

How Much Do I Want To Make In Revenue Weekly?

How Much Do I Want To Make In Revenue Monthly?

How Much Do I Want To Make In Revenue Quarterly?

How Much Do I Want To Make In Revenue Yearly?

How Much Does It Cost To Run My Business Monthly?

Running The Numbers

My Future Projections Are:

My Future Projections Are Based Off Of:

How Much Of Each Sale Will Go Towards Savings And Reinvestment?

How Much Debt Does The Business Currently Have (Answer If Applicable)?

How Much Debt Will My Business Have Within The Next Month?

Running The Numbers

How Much Debt Will My Business Have Within The Next Quarter?

How Much Debt Will My Business Have Within The Next Year?

How Many Sales Do I Need Each Day To Reach My Goals?

How Many Customers Need To See My Product(s)/Service(s) Each Day To Reach My Daily Goals?

What Is My Net Profit Margin With Each Product/Service?

Running The Numbers

What Is My Gross Profit Margin With Each Product/Service?

What Kind Of ROI (Return On Investment) Is Needed Daily To Reach My Daily Goals?

In Two Years My Business Will Be Making?

In Five Years My Business Will Be Making?

In Ten Years My Business Will Be Making?

Running The Numbers

What Percentage Of My Sales Come From Online?

What Percentage Of My Sales Come From My Physical Location And/Or Offline Marketing Efforts?

What Is The Online Marketing Budget?

What Is The Offline Marketing Budget?

What Is The Product Production Budget?

Running The Numbers

What Is The Employee Payroll Budget?

What Is The Budget For Packaging?

What Is The Budget For Website Maintenance?

What Is The Budget For Business Travel?

What Is The Budget For Business Events?

Running The Numbers

What Are My Brick And Mortar Operating Expenses (Answer If Applicable)?

Running The Numbers

Sales Forecast

A Continuation Of My Sales Forecast

Running The Numbers

Expense Budget

A Continuation Of My Expense Budget

Running The Numbers

Income Projections For The Next Twelve Months

A Continuation Of My Income Projections For The Next Twelve Months

Running The Numbers

Breakeven Analysis

A Continuation Of My Breakeven Analysis

My Business Inspirations

My Business Inspirations....

Business Minded Daily

Business Minded Daily

Date: Mood:

Morning Thoughts

Today's Affirmation: I Am Creating:

My Motivation: Today I Will Not Forget To:

I Will Push Through: Spiritual/Mental/Physical Work That Will
                                         Be Done Today:

Nightly Thoughts

Time: I Feel:

Today's Accomplishment: Today I Had To Change:

I Believe: I Spent Time Learning:

Today's Challenges: I Connected With:

Today My Business Needed: I Sharpened My Skills/Products By:

145

I Love Being An Entrepreneur.

Business Minded Daily

Date: Mood:

Morning Thoughts

Today's Affirmation: I Am Creating:

My Motivation: Today I Will Not Forget To:

I Will Push Through: Spiritual/Mental/Physical Work That Will
                                         Be Done Today:

Nightly Thoughts

Time: I Feel:

Today's Accomplishment: Today I Had To Change:

I Believe: I Spent Time Learning:

Today's Challenges: I Connected With:

Today My Business Needed: I Sharpened My Skills/Products By:

My Business Notes

Business Minded Daily

Date: Mood:

Morning Thoughts

Today's Affirmation: I Am Creating:

My Motivation: Today I Will Not Forget To:

I Will Push Through: Spiritual/Mental/Physical Work That Will
                                         Be Done Today:

Nightly Thoughts

Time: I Feel:

Today's Accomplishment: Today I Had To Change:

I Believe: I Spent Time Learning:

Today's Challenges: I Connected With:

Today My Business Needed: I Sharpened My Skills/Products By:

Business Minded Daily

Date: Mood:

Morning Thoughts

Today's Affirmation: | I Am Creating:

My Motivation: | Today I Will Not Forget To:

I Will Push Through: | Spiritual/Mental/Physical Work That Will Be Done Today:

Nightly Thoughts

Time: | I Feel:

Today's Accomplishment: | Today I Had To Change:

I Believe: | I Spent Time Learning:

Today's Challenges: | I Connected With:

Today My Business Needed: | I Sharpened My Skills/Products By:

I Minded My Own Business And Created My Own Business.

Business Minded Daily

Date: Mood:

Morning Thoughts

Today's Affirmation: I Am Creating:

My Motivation: Today I Will Not Forget To:

I Will Push Through: Spiritual/Mental/Physical Work That Will
                                         Be Done Today:

Nightly Thoughts

Time: I Feel:

Today's Accomplishment: Today I Had To Change:

I Believe: I Spent Time Learning:

Today's Challenges: I Connected With:

Today My Business Needed: I Sharpened My Skills/Products By:

Business Minded Daily

Date: Mood:

Morning Thoughts

Today's Affirmation: I Am Creating:

My Motivation: Today I Will Not Forget To:

I Will Push Through: Spiritual/Mental/Physical Work That Will
                               Be Done Today:

Nightly Thoughts

Time: I Feel:

Today's Accomplishment: Today I Had To Change:

I Believe: I Spent Time Learning:

Today's Challenges: I Connected With:

Today My Business Needed: I Sharpened My Skills/Products By:

I Will Conquer Every Business Challenge.

Business Minded Daily

Date: Mood:

Morning Thoughts

Today's Affirmation: I Am Creating:

My Motivation: Today I Will Not Forget To:

I Will Push Through: Spiritual/Mental/Physical Work That Will
                                         Be Done Today:

Nightly Thoughts

Time: I Feel:

Today's Accomplishment: Today I Had To Change:

I Believe: I Spent Time Learning:

Today's Challenges: I Connected With:

Today My Business Needed: I Sharpened My Skills/Products By:

My Business Notes

Business Minded Daily

Date: Mood:

Morning Thoughts

Today's Affirmation: I Am Creating:

My Motivation: Today I Will Not Forget To:

I Will Push Through: Spiritual/Mental/Physical Work That Will
                                         Be Done Today:

Nightly Thoughts

Time: I Feel:

Today's Accomplishment: Today I Had To Change:

I Believe: I Spent Time Learning:

Today's Challenges: I Connected With:

Today My Business Needed: I Sharpened My Skills/Products By:

Business Minded Daily

Date: Mood:

Morning Thoughts

Today's Affirmation: I Am Creating:

My Motivation: Today I Will Not Forget To:

I Will Push Through: Spiritual/Mental/Physical Work That Will
                                                   Be Done Today:

Nightly Thoughts

Time: I Feel:

Today's Accomplishment: Today I Had To Change:

I Believe: I Spent Time Learning:

Today's Challenges: I Connected With:

Today My Business Needed: I Sharpened My Skills/Products By:

My Business Is A Representation Of Me.

Business Minded Daily

Date: Mood:

Morning Thoughts

Today's Affirmation: I Am Creating:

My Motivation: Today I Will Not Forget To:

I Will Push Through: Spiritual/Mental/Physical Work That Will
                                         Be Done Today:

Nightly Thoughts

Time: I Feel:

Today's Accomplishment: Today I Had To Change:

I Believe: I Spent Time Learning:

Today's Challenges: I Connected With:

Today My Business Needed: I Sharpened My Skills/Products By:

160

I Work Hard
And Smart For
Myself And
Others.

Business Minded Daily

Date: Mood:

Morning Thoughts

Today's Affirmation: I Am Creating:

My Motivation: Today I Will Not Forget To:

I Will Push Through: Spiritual/Mental/Physical Work That Will
                                        Be Done Today:

Nightly Thoughts

Time: I Feel:

Today's Accomplishment: Today I Had To Change:

I Believe: I Spent Time Learning:

Today's Challenges: I Connected With:

Today My Business Needed: I Sharpened My Skills/Products By:

162

My Business Aligns With My Values.

Business Minded Daily

Date: Mood:

Morning Thoughts

Today's Affirmation: I Am Creating:

My Motivation: Today I Will Not Forget To:

I Will Push Through: Spiritual/Mental/Physical Work That Will
                                         Be Done Today:

Nightly Thoughts

Time: I Feel:

Today's Accomplishment: Today I Had To Change:

I Believe: I Spent Time Learning:

Today's Challenges: I Connected With:

Today My Business Needed: I Sharpened My Skills/Products By:

My Business Notes

Business Minded Daily

Date: Mood:

Morning Thoughts

Today's Affirmation: I Am Creating:

My Motivation: Today I Will Not Forget To:

I Will Push Through: Spiritual/Mental/Physical Work That Will
                                               Be Done Today:

Nightly Thoughts

Time: I Feel:

Today's Accomplishment: Today I Had To Change:

I Believe: I Spent Time Learning:

Today's Challenges: I Connected With:

Today My Business Needed: I Sharpened My Skills/Products By:

I Will Create The Opportunity.

Business Minded Daily

Date: Mood:

Morning Thoughts

Today's Affirmation: I Am Creating:

My Motivation: Today I Will Not Forget To:

I Will Push Through: Spiritual/Mental/Physical Work That Will
                                         Be Done Today:

Nightly Thoughts

Time: I Feel:

Today's Accomplishment: Today I Had To Change:

I Believe: I Spent Time Learning:

Today's Challenges: I Connected With:

Today My Business Needed: I Sharpened My Skills/Products By:

Business Minded Daily

Date: Mood:

Morning Thoughts

Today's Affirmation: I Am Creating:

My Motivation: Today I Will Not Forget To:

I Will Push Through: Spiritual/Mental/Physical Work That Will
                                     Be Done Today:

Nightly Thoughts

Time: I Feel:

Today's Accomplishment: Today I Had To Change:

I Believe: I Spent Time Learning:

Today's Challenges: I Connected With:

Today My Business Needed: I Sharpened My Skills/Products By:

169

Business Minded Daily

Date: Mood:

Morning Thoughts

Today's Affirmation: I Am Creating:

My Motivation: Today I Will Not Forget To:

I Will Push Through: Spiritual/Mental/Physical Work That Will
                                           Be Done Today:

Nightly Thoughts

Time: I Feel:

Today's Accomplishment: Today I Had To Change:

I Believe: I Spent Time Learning:

Today's Challenges: I Connected With:

Today My Business Needed: I Sharpened My Skills/Products By:

Business Minded Daily

Date: Mood:

Morning Thoughts

Today's Affirmation: I Am Creating:

My Motivation: Today I Will Not Forget To:

I Will Push Through: Spiritual/Mental/Physical Work That Will
                                         Be Done Today:

Nightly Thoughts

Time: I Feel:

Today's Accomplishment: Today I Had To Change:

I Believe: I Spent Time Learning:

Today's Challenges: I Connected With:

Today My Business Needed: I Sharpened My Skills/Products By:

My Business Heals. My Business Makes Life Easier.

Business Minded Daily

Date: Mood:

Morning Thoughts

Today's Affirmation: I Am Creating:

My Motivation: Today I Will Not Forget To:

I Will Push Through: Spiritual/Mental/Physical Work That Will
                               Be Done Today:

Nightly Thoughts

Time: I Feel:

Today's Accomplishment: Today I Had To Change:

I Believe: I Spent Time Learning:

Today's Challenges: I Connected With:

Today My Business Needed: I Sharpened My Skills/Products By:

My Business Notes

Business Minded Daily

Date: Mood:

Morning Thoughts

Today's Affirmation: I Am Creating:

My Motivation: Today I Will Not Forget To:

I Will Push Through: Spiritual/Mental/Physical Work That Will
                                         Be Done Today:

Nightly Thoughts

Time: I Feel:

Today's Accomplishment: Today I Had To Change:

I Believe: I Spent Time Learning:

Today's Challenges: I Connected With:

Today My Business Needed: I Sharpened My Skills/Products By:

Business Minded Daily

Date: Mood:

Morning Thoughts

Today's Affirmation: I Am Creating:

My Motivation: Today I Will Not Forget To:

I Will Push Through: Spiritual/Mental/Physical Work That Will
                                         Be Done Today:

Nightly Thoughts

Time: I Feel:

Today's Accomplishment: Today I Had To Change:

I Believe: I Spent Time Learning:

Today's Challenges: I Connected With:

Today My Business Needed: I Sharpened My Skills/Products By:

They Told Me It Wouldn't Work.

Now They See It Working.

Business Minded Daily

Date: Mood:

Morning Thoughts

Today's Affirmation: I Am Creating:

My Motivation: Today I Will Not Forget To:

I Will Push Through: Spiritual/Mental/Physical Work That Will
                                           Be Done Today:

Nightly Thoughts

Time: I Feel:

Today's Accomplishment: Today I Had To Change:

I Believe: I Spent Time Learning:

Today's Challenges: I Connected With:

Today My Business Needed: I Sharpened My Skills/Products By:

Business Minded Daily

Date: Mood:

Morning Thoughts

Today's Affirmation: I Am Creating:

My Motivation: Today I Will Not Forget To:

I Will Push Through: Spiritual/Mental/Physical Work That Will
                                         Be Done Today:

Nightly Thoughts

Time: I Feel:

Today's Accomplishment: Today I Had To Change:

I Believe: I Spent Time Learning:

Today's Challenges: I Connected With:

Today My Business Needed: I Sharpened My Skills/Products By:

Business Minded Daily

Date: Mood:

Morning Thoughts

Today's Affirmation: I Am Creating:

My Motivation: Today I Will Not Forget To:

I Will Push Through: Spiritual/Mental/Physical Work That Will
                                         Be Done Today:

Nightly Thoughts

Time: I Feel:

Today's Accomplishment: Today I Had To Change:

I Believe: I Spent Time Learning:

Today's Challenges: I Connected With:

Today My Business Needed: I Sharpened My Skills/Products By:

180

I Feel Good About What I Am Working On.

Business Minded Daily

Date: Mood:

Morning Thoughts

Today's Affirmation: I Am Creating:

My Motivation: Today I Will Not Forget To:

I Will Push Through: Spiritual/Mental/Physical Work That Will
                                         Be Done Today:

Nightly Thoughts

Time: I Feel:

Today's Accomplishment: Today I Had To Change:

I Believe: I Spent Time Learning:

Today's Challenges: I Connected With:

Today My Business Needed: I Sharpened My Skills/Products By:

My Business Notes

Business Minded Daily

Date: Mood:

Morning Thoughts

Today's Affirmation: I Am Creating:

My Motivation: Today I Will Not Forget To:

I Will Push Through: Spiritual/Mental/Physical Work That Will
                                         Be Done Today:

Nightly Thoughts

Time: I Feel:

Today's Accomplishment: Today I Had To Change:

I Believe: I Spent Time Learning:

Today's Challenges: I Connected With:

Today My Business Needed: I Sharpened My Skills/Products By:

Business Minded Daily

Date: Mood:

Morning Thoughts

Today's Affirmation: I Am Creating:

My Motivation: Today I Will Not Forget To:

I Will Push Through: Spiritual/Mental/Physical Work That Will
                                         Be Done Today:

Nightly Thoughts

Time: I Feel:

Today's Accomplishment: Today I Had To Change:

I Believe: I Spent Time Learning:

Today's Challenges: I Connected With:

Today My Business Needed: I Sharpened My Skills/Products By:

Business Minded Daily

Date: Mood:

Morning Thoughts

Today's Affirmation: I Am Creating:

My Motivation: Today I Will Not Forget To:

I Will Push Through: Spiritual/Mental/Physical Work That Will
                                         Be Done Today:

Nightly Thoughts

Time: I Feel:

Today's Accomplishment: Today I Had To Change:

I Believe: I Spent Time Learning:

Today's Challenges: I Connected With:

Today My Business Needed: I Sharpened My Skills/Products By:

I Create Goals Then I Achieve Them.

Business Minded Daily

Date: Mood:

Morning Thoughts

Today's Affirmation: I Am Creating:

My Motivation: Today I Will Not Forget To:

I Will Push Through: Spiritual/Mental/Physical Work That Will
                                         Be Done Today:

Nightly Thoughts

Time: I Feel:

Today's Accomplishment: Today I Had To Change:

I Believe: I Spent Time Learning:

Today's Challenges: I Connected With:

Today My Business Needed: I Sharpened My Skills/Products By:

Business Minded Daily

Date: Mood:

Morning Thoughts

Today's Affirmation: I Am Creating:

My Motivation: Today I Will Not Forget To:

I Will Push Through: Spiritual/Mental/Physical Work That Will
                                               Be Done Today:

Nightly Thoughts

Time: I Feel:

Today's Accomplishment: Today I Had To Change:

I Believe: I Spent Time Learning:

Today's Challenges: I Connected With:

Today My Business Needed: I Sharpened My Skills/Products By:

Business Minded Daily

Date: Mood:

Morning Thoughts

Today's Affirmation: I Am Creating:

My Motivation: Today I Will Not Forget To:

I Will Push Through: Spiritual/Mental/Physical Work That Will
                                             Be Done Today:

Nightly Thoughts

Time: I Feel:

Today's Accomplishment: Today I Had To Change:

I Believe: I Spent Time Learning:

Today's Challenges: I Connected With:

Today My Business Needed: I Sharpened My Skills/Products By:

Even When It Feels Like I Should Give Up, I Know That This Feeling Is The Turning Point To Success.

Business Minded Daily

Date: Mood:

Morning Thoughts

Today's Affirmation: I Am Creating:

My Motivation: Today I Will Not Forget To:

I Will Push Through: Spiritual/Mental/Physical Work That Will
                                               Be Done Today:

Nightly Thoughts

Time: I Feel:

Today's Accomplishment: Today I Had To Change:

I Believe: I Spent Time Learning:

Today's Challenges: I Connected With:

Today My Business Needed: I Sharpened My Skills/Products By:

Business Minded Daily

Date: Mood:

Morning Thoughts

Today's Affirmation: I Am Creating:

My Motivation: Today I Will Not Forget To:

I Will Push Through: Spiritual/Mental/Physical Work That Will
                                         Be Done Today:

Nightly Thoughts

Time: I Feel:

Today's Accomplishment: Today I Had To Change:

I Believe: I Spent Time Learning:

Today's Challenges: I Connected With:

Today My Business Needed: I Sharpened My Skills/Products By:

My Business Notes

Business Minded Daily

Date: Mood:

Morning Thoughts

Today's Affirmation: I Am Creating:

My Motivation: Today I Will Not Forget To:

I Will Push Through: Spiritual/Mental/Physical Work That Will
                                         Be Done Today:

Nightly Thoughts

Time: I Feel:

Today's Accomplishment: Today I Had To Change:

I Believe: I Spent Time Learning:

Today's Challenges: I Connected With:

Today My Business Needed: I Sharpened My Skills/Products By:

The Journey I Am
Taking Is Not One
Everyone Will Want
To Take With Me.

Business Minded Daily

Date: Mood:

Morning Thoughts

Today's Affirmation: I Am Creating:

My Motivation: Today I Will Not Forget To:

I Will Push Through: Spiritual/Mental/Physical Work That Will
                                         Be Done Today:

Nightly Thoughts

Time: I Feel:

Today's Accomplishment: Today I Had To Change:

I Believe: I Spent Time Learning:

Today's Challenges: I Connected With:

Today My Business Needed: I Sharpened My Skills/Products By:

Business Minded Daily

Date: Mood:

Morning Thoughts

Today's Affirmation: I Am Creating:

My Motivation: Today I Will Not Forget To:

I Will Push Through: Spiritual/Mental/Physical Work That Will
                                         Be Done Today:

Nightly Thoughts

Time: I Feel:

Today's Accomplishment: Today I Had To Change:

I Believe: I Spent Time Learning:

Today's Challenges: I Connected With:

Today My Business Needed: I Sharpened My Skills/Products By:

Business Minded Daily

Date: Mood:

Morning Thoughts

Today's Affirmation: I Am Creating:

My Motivation: Today I Will Not Forget To:

I Will Push Through: Spiritual/Mental/Physical Work That Will Be Done Today:

Nightly Thoughts

Time: I Feel:

Today's Accomplishment: Today I Had To Change:

I Believe: I Spent Time Learning:

Today's Challenges: I Connected With:

Today My Business Needed: I Sharpened My Skills/Products By:

Business Minded Daily

Date: Mood:

Morning Thoughts

Today's Affirmation: I Am Creating:

My Motivation: Today I Will Not Forget To:

I Will Push Through: Spiritual/Mental/Physical Work That Will
                                        Be Done Today:

Nightly Thoughts

Time: I Feel:

Today's Accomplishment: Today I Had To Change:

I Believe: I Spent Time Learning:

Today's Challenges: I Connected With:

Today My Business Needed: I Sharpened My Skills/Products By:

200

My Work
Ethic Is
Unbeatable.

Business Minded Daily

Date: Mood:

Morning Thoughts

Today's Affirmation: I Am Creating:

My Motivation: Today I Will Not Forget To:

I Will Push Through: Spiritual/Mental/Physical Work That Will
                                         Be Done Today:

Nightly Thoughts

Time: I Feel:

Today's Accomplishment: Today I Had To Change:

I Believe: I Spent Time Learning:

Today's Challenges: I Connected With:

Today My Business Needed: I Sharpened My Skills/Products By:

I Have A Purpose.

Business Minded Daily

Date: Mood:

Morning Thoughts

Today's Affirmation: I Am Creating:

My Motivation: Today I Will Not Forget To:

I Will Push Through: Spiritual/Mental/Physical Work That Will
                                         Be Done Today:

Nightly Thoughts

Time: I Feel:

Today's Accomplishment: Today I Had To Change:

I Believe: I Spent Time Learning:

Today's Challenges: I Connected With:

Today My Business Needed: I Sharpened My Skills/Products By:

My Business Notes

Business Minded Daily

Date: Mood:

Morning Thoughts

Today's Affirmation: I Am Creating:

My Motivation: Today I Will Not Forget To:

I Will Push Through: Spiritual/Mental/Physical Work That Will
                                           Be Done Today:

Nightly Thoughts

Time: I Feel:

Today's Accomplishment: Today I Had To Change:

I Believe: I Spent Time Learning:

Today's Challenges: I Connected With:

Today My Business Needed: I Sharpened My Skills/Products By:

Business Minded Daily

Date: _____   Mood: _____

Morning Thoughts

Today's Affirmation:

My Motivation:

I Will Push Through:

I Am Creating:

Today I Will Not Forget To:

Spiritual/Mental/Physical Work That Will Be Done Today:

Nightly Thoughts

Time:

Today's Accomplishment:

I Believe:

Today's Challenges:

Today My Business Needed:

I Feel:

Today I Had To Change:

I Spent Time Learning:

I Connected With:

I Sharpened My Skills/Products By:

Business Minded Daily

Date: Mood:

Morning Thoughts

Today's Affirmation: I Am Creating:

My Motivation: Today I Will Not Forget To:

I Will Push Through: Spiritual/Mental/Physical Work That Will
                                         Be Done Today:

Nightly Thoughts

Time: I Feel:

Today's Accomplishment: Today I Had To Change:

I Believe: I Spent Time Learning:

Today's Challenges: I Connected With:

Today My Business Needed: I Sharpened My Skills/Products By:

There Is Something Empowering About Creating Something From The Ground Up.

Business Minded Daily

Date: Mood:

Morning Thoughts

Today's Affirmation: I Am Creating:

My Motivation: Today I Will Not Forget To:

I Will Push Through: Spiritual/Mental/Physical Work That Will Be Done Today:

Nightly Thoughts

Time: I Feel:

Today's Accomplishment: Today I Had To Change:

I Believe: I Spent Time Learning:

Today's Challenges: I Connected With:

Today My Business Needed: I Sharpened My Skills/Products By:

Business Minded Daily

Date: Mood:

Morning Thoughts

Today's Affirmation: I Am Creating:

My Motivation: Today I Will Not Forget To:

I Will Push Through: Spiritual/Mental/Physical Work That Will Be Done Today:

Nightly Thoughts

Time: I Feel:

Today's Accomplishment: Today I Had To Change:

I Believe: I Spent Time Learning:

Today's Challenges: I Connected With:

Today My Business Needed: I Sharpened My Skills/Products By:

My Business Notes

Business Minded Daily

Date: Mood:

Morning Thoughts

Today's Affirmation: I Am Creating:

My Motivation: Today I Will Not Forget To:

I Will Push Through: Spiritual/Mental/Physical Work That Will
                                         Be Done Today:

Nightly Thoughts

Time: I Feel:

Today's Accomplishment: Today I Had To Change:

I Believe: I Spent Time Learning:

Today's Challenges: I Connected With:

Today My Business Needed: I Sharpened My Skills/Products By:

If Something Does Not
Work, Never Change
Th Target .... Just
Change How You Aim.

Business Minded Daily

Date: Mood:

Morning Thoughts

Today's Affirmation: I Am Creating:

My Motivation: Today I Will Not Forget To:

I Will Push Through: Spiritual/Mental/Physical Work That Will
                                        Be Done Today:

Nightly Thoughts

Time: I Feel:

Today's Accomplishment: Today I Had To Change:

I Believe: I Spent Time Learning:

Today's Challenges: I Connected With:

Today My Business Needed: I Sharpened My Skills/Products By:

My Business Notes

Business Minded Daily

Date: _____   Mood: _____

Morning Thoughts

Today's Affirmation: I Am Creating:

My Motivation: Today I Will Not Forget To:

I Will Push Through: Spiritual/Mental/Physical Work That Will
                                  Be Done Today:

Nightly Thoughts

Time: I Feel:

Today's Accomplishment: Today I Had To Change:

I Believe: I Spent Time Learning:

Today's Challenges: I Connected With:

Today My Business Needed: I Sharpened My Skills/Products By:

Business Minded Daily

Date: Mood:

Morning Thoughts

Today's Affirmation: I Am Creating:

My Motivation: Today I Will Not Forget To:

I Will Push Through: Spiritual/Mental/Physical Work That Will
                                         Be Done Today:

Nightly Thoughts

Time: I Feel:

Today's Accomplishment: Today I Had To Change:

I Believe: I Spent Time Learning:

Today's Challenges: I Connected With:

Today My Business Needed: I Sharpened My Skills/Products By:

218

Business Minded Daily

Date: Mood:

Morning Thoughts

Today's Affirmation: I Am Creating:

My Motivation: Today I Will Not Forget To:

I Will Push Through: Spiritual/Mental/Physical Work That Will
                                         Be Done Today:

Nightly Thoughts

Time: I Feel:

Today's Accomplishment: Today I Had To Change:

I Believe: I Spent Time Learning:

Today's Challenges: I Connected With:

Today My Business Needed: I Sharpened My Skills/Products By:

You Have Got To Be Willing To Take Some Risk.

Business Minded Daily

Date: Mood:

Morning Thoughts

Today's Affirmation: I Am Creating:

My Motivation: Today I Will Not Forget To:

I Will Push Through: Spiritual/Mental/Physical Work That Will
                                               Be Done Today:

Nightly Thoughts

Time: I Feel:

Today's Accomplishment: Today I Had To Change:

I Believe: I Spent Time Learning:

Today's Challenges: I Connected With:

Today My Business Needed: I Sharpened My Skills/Products By:

My Business Notes

Business Minded Daily

Date: Mood:

Morning Thoughts

Today's Affirmation: I Am Creating:

My Motivation: Today I Will Not Forget To:

I Will Push Through: Spiritual/Mental/Physical Work That Will
                                         Be Done Today:

Nightly Thoughts

Time: I Feel:

Today's Accomplishment: Today I Had To Change:

I Believe: I Spent Time Learning:

Today's Challenges: I Connected With:

Today My Business Needed: I Sharpened My Skills/Products By:

Business Minded Daily

Date: Mood:

Morning Thoughts

Today's Affirmation: I Am Creating:

My Motivation: Today I Will Not Forget To:

I Will Push Through: Spiritual/Mental/Physical Work That Will
                                         Be Done Today:

Nightly Thoughts

Time: I Feel:

Today's Accomplishment: Today I Had To Change:

I Believe: I Spent Time Learning:

Today's Challenges: I Connected With:

Today My Business Needed: I Sharpened My Skills/Products By:

Business Minded Daily

Date: Mood:

Morning Thoughts

Today's Affirmation: I Am Creating:

My Motivation: Today I Will Not Forget To:

I Will Push Through: Spiritual/Mental/Physical Work That Will
                                         Be Done Today:

Nightly Thoughts

Time: I Feel:

Today's Accomplishment: Today I Had To Change:

I Believe: I Spent Time Learning:

Today's Challenges: I Connected With:

Today My Business Needed: I Sharpened My Skills/Products By:

Success

Is

Inevitable.

Business Minded Daily

Date: Mood:

Morning Thoughts

Today's Affirmation: I Am Creating:

My Motivation: Today I Will Not Forget To:

I Will Push Through: Spiritual/Mental/Physical Work That Will
                                               Be Done Today:

Nightly Thoughts

Time: I Feel:

Today's Accomplishment: Today I Had To Change:

I Believe: I Spent Time Learning:

Today's Challenges: I Connected With:

Today My Business Needed: I Sharpened My Skills/Products By:

Business Minded Daily

Date: Mood:

Morning Thoughts

Today's Affirmation: I Am Creating:

My Motivation: Today I Will Not Forget To:

I Will Push Through: Spiritual/Mental/Physical Work That Will
                                         Be Done Today:

Nightly Thoughts

Time: I Feel:

Today's Accomplishment: Today I Had To Change:

I Believe: I Spent Time Learning:

Today's Challenges: I Connected With:

Today My Business Needed: I Sharpened My Skills/Products By:

228

Business Minded Daily

Date: Mood:

Morning Thoughts

Today's Affirmation: I Am Creating:

My Motivation: Today I Will Not Forget To:

I Will Push Through: Spiritual/Mental/Physical Work That Will
                                         Be Done Today:

Nightly Thoughts

Time: I Feel:

Today's Accomplishment: Today I Had To Change:

I Believe: I Spent Time Learning:

Today's Challenges: I Connected With:

Today My Business Needed: I Sharpened My Skills/Products By:

Business Minded Daily

Date: Mood:

Morning Thoughts

Today's Affirmation: I Am Creating:

My Motivation: Today I Will Not Forget To:

I Will Push Through: Spiritual/Mental/Physical Work That Will
                                               Be Done Today:

Nightly Thoughts

Time: I Feel:

Today's Accomplishment: Today I Had To Change:

I Believe: I Spent Time Learning:

Today's Challenges: I Connected With:

Today My Business Needed: I Sharpened My Skills/Products By:

230

A Successful Business Requires A Team.

Business Minded Daily

Date: Mood:

Morning Thoughts

Today's Affirmation: I Am Creating:

My Motivation: Today I Will Not Forget To:

I Will Push Through: Spiritual/Mental/Physical Work That Will
                                               Be Done Today:

Nightly Thoughts

Time: I Feel:

Today's Accomplishment: Today I Had To Change:

I Believe: I Spent Time Learning:

Today's Challenges: I Connected With:

Today My Business Needed: I Sharpened My Skills/Products By:

I No Longer

Wish.

I Just Do.

Business Minded Daily

Date: Mood:

Morning Thoughts

Today's Affirmation: I Am Creating:

My Motivation: Today I Will Not Forget To:

I Will Push Through: Spiritual/Mental/Physical Work That Will
                                         Be Done Today:

Nightly Thoughts

Time: I Feel:

Today's Accomplishment: Today I Had To Change:

I Believe: I Spent Time Learning:

Today's Challenges: I Connected With:

Today My Business Needed: I Sharpened My Skills/Products By:

My Business Notes

Business Minded Daily

Date: Mood:

Morning Thoughts

Today's Affirmation: I Am Creating:

My Motivation: Today I Will Not Forget To:

I Will Push Through: Spiritual/Mental/Physical Work That Will
                                               Be Done Today:

Nightly Thoughts

Time: I Feel:

Today's Accomplishment: Today I Had To Change:

I Believe: I Spent Time Learning:

Today's Challenges: I Connected With:

Today My Business Needed: I Sharpened My Skills/Products By:

Business Minded Daily

Date: Mood:

Morning Thoughts

Today's Affirmation: I Am Creating:

My Motivation: Today I Will Not Forget To:

I Will Push Through: Spiritual/Mental/Physical Work That Will
                                                Be Done Today:

Nightly Thoughts

Time: I Feel:

Today's Accomplishment: Today I Had To Change:

I Believe: I Spent Time Learning:

Today's Challenges: I Connected With:

Today My Business Needed: I Sharpened My Skills/Products By:

Business Minded Daily

Date: Mood:

Morning Thoughts

Today's Affirmation: I Am Creating:

My Motivation: Today I Will Not Forget To:

I Will Push Through: Spiritual/Mental/Physical Work That Will
                                        Be Done Today:

Nightly Thoughts

Time: I Feel:

Today's Accomplishment: Today I Had To Change:

I Believe: I Spent Time Learning:

Today's Challenges: I Connected With:

Today My Business Needed: I Sharpened My Skills/Products By:

Watch Me Make

Something Out

Of Nothing.

Business Minded Daily

Date: Mood:

Morning Thoughts

Today's Affirmation: I Am Creating:

My Motivation: Today I Will Not Forget To:

I Will Push Through: Spiritual/Mental/Physical Work That Will
                                         Be Done Today:

Nightly Thoughts

Time: I Feel:

Today's Accomplishment: Today I Had To Change:

I Believe: I Spent Time Learning:

Today's Challenges: I Connected With:

Today My Business Needed: I Sharpened My Skills/Products By:

Business Minded Daily

Date: Mood:

Morning Thoughts

Today's Affirmation:

My Motivation:

I Will Push Through:

I Am Creating:

Today I Will Not Forget To:

Spiritual/Mental/Physical Work That Will Be Done Today:

Nightly Thoughts

Time:

Today's Accomplishment:

I Believe:

Today's Challenges:

Today My Business Needed:

I Feel:

Today I Had To Change:

I Spent Time Learning:

I Connected With:

I Sharpened My Skills/Products By:

My Business Notes

Business Minded Daily

Date: Mood:

Morning Thoughts

Today's Affirmation: I Am Creating:

My Motivation: Today I Will Not Forget To:

I Will Push Through: Spiritual/Mental/Physical Work That Will
                                         Be Done Today:

Nightly Thoughts

Time: I Feel:

Today's Accomplishment: Today I Had To Change:

I Believe: I Spent Time Learning:

Today's Challenges: I Connected With:

Today My Business Needed: I Sharpened My Skills/Products By:

Business Minded Daily

Date: Mood:

Morning Thoughts

Today's Affirmation: I Am Creating:

My Motivation: Today I Will Not Forget To:

I Will Push Through: Spiritual/Mental/Physical Work That Will
                                         Be Done Today:

Nightly Thoughts

Time: I Feel:

Today's Accomplishment: Today I Had To Change:

I Believe: I Spent Time Learning:

Today's Challenges: I Connected With:

Today My Business Needed: I Sharpened My Skills/Products By:

Business Minded Daily

Date: Mood:

Morning Thoughts

Today's Affirmation: I Am Creating:

My Motivation: Today I Will Not Forget To:

I Will Push Through: Spiritual/Mental/Physical Work That Will
                                         Be Done Today:

Nightly Thoughts

Time: I Feel:

Today's Accomplishment: Today I Had To Change:

I Believe: I Spent Time Learning:

Today's Challenges: I Connected With:

Today My Business Needed: I Sharpened My Skills/Products By:

I Am The Game Changer.

Business Minded Daily

Date: Mood:

Morning Thoughts

Today's Affirmation: I Am Creating:

My Motivation: Today I Will Not Forget To:

I Will Push Through: Spiritual/Mental/Physical Work That Will
                                         Be Done Today:

Nightly Thoughts

Time: I Feel:

Today's Accomplishment: Today I Had To Change:

I Believe: I Spent Time Learning:

Today's Challenges: I Connected With:

Today My Business Needed: I Sharpened My Skills/Products By:

Business Minded Daily

Date: Mood:

Morning Thoughts

Today's Affirmation: I Am Creating:

My Motivation: Today I Will Not Forget To:

I Will Push Through: Spiritual/Mental/Physical Work That Will
                                               Be Done Today:

Nightly Thoughts

Time: I Feel:

Today's Accomplishment: Today I Had To Change:

I Believe: I Spent Time Learning:

Today's Challenges: I Connected With:

Today My Business Needed: I Sharpened My Skills/Products By:

My Business Notes

Business Minded Daily

Date: Mood:

Morning Thoughts

Today's Affirmation: I Am Creating:

My Motivation: Today I Will Not Forget To:

I Will Push Through: Spiritual/Mental/Physical Work That Will
                                           Be Done Today:

Nightly Thoughts

Time: I Feel:

Today's Accomplishment: Today I Had To Change:

I Believe: I Spent Time Learning:

Today's Challenges: I Connected With:

Today My Business Needed: I Sharpened My Skills/Products By:

250

Business Minded Daily

Date: Mood:

Morning Thoughts

Today's Affirmation: I Am Creating:

My Motivation: Today I Will Not Forget To:

I Will Push Through: Spiritual/Mental/Physical Work That Will
                                Be Done Today:

Nightly Thoughts

Time: I Feel:

Today's Accomplishment: Today I Had To Change:

I Believe: I Spent Time Learning:

Today's Challenges: I Connected With:

Today My Business Needed: I Sharpened My Skills/Products By:

My Brand Is Bigger Than Me.

Business Minded Daily

Date: Mood:

Morning Thoughts

Today's Affirmation: I Am Creating:

My Motivation: Today I Will Not Forget To:

I Will Push Through: Spiritual/Mental/Physical Work That Will
                               Be Done Today:

Nightly Thoughts

Time: I Feel:

Today's Accomplishment: Today I Had To Change:

I Believe: I Spent Time Learning:

Today's Challenges: I Connected With:

Today My Business Needed: I Sharpened My Skills/Products By:

Business Minded Daily

Date: Mood:

Morning Thoughts

Today's Affirmation: I Am Creating:

My Motivation: Today I Will Not Forget To:

I Will Push Through: Spiritual/Mental/Physical Work That Will
                                         Be Done Today:

Nightly Thoughts

Time: I Feel:

Today's Accomplishment: Today I Had To Change:

I Believe: I Spent Time Learning:

Today's Challenges: I Connected With:

Today My Business Needed: I Sharpened My Skills/Products By:

Business Minded Daily

Date: Mood:

Morning Thoughts

Today's Affirmation: I Am Creating:

My Motivation: Today I Will Not Forget To:

I Will Push Through: Spiritual/Mental/Physical Work That Will
                                         Be Done Today:

Nightly Thoughts

Time: I Feel:

Today's Accomplishment: Today I Had To Change:

I Believe: I Spent Time Learning:

Today's Challenges: I Connected With:

Today My Business Needed: I Sharpened My Skills/Products By:

Business Minded Daily

Date: Mood:

Morning Thoughts

Today's Affirmation: I Am Creating:

My Motivation: Today I Will Not Forget To:

I Will Push Through: Spiritual/Mental/Physical Work That Will
                                         Be Done Today:

Nightly Thoughts

Time: I Feel:

Today's Accomplishment: Today I Had To Change:

I Believe: I Spent Time Learning:

Today's Challenges: I Connected With:

Today My Business Needed: I Sharpened My Skills/Products By:

256

I Set The Goal, Then I Conquer It.

Business Minded Daily

Date: Mood:

Morning Thoughts

Today's Affirmation: I Am Creating:

My Motivation: Today I Will Not Forget To:

I Will Push Through: Spiritual/Mental/Physical Work That Will
                                         Be Done Today:

Nightly Thoughts

Time: I Feel:

Today's Accomplishment: Today I Had To Change:

I Believe: I Spent Time Learning:

Today's Challenges: I Connected With:

Today My Business Needed: I Sharpened My Skills/Products By:

258

My Business Notes

Business Minded Daily

Date: Mood:

Morning Thoughts

Today's Affirmation: I Am Creating:

My Motivation: Today I Will Not Forget To:

I Will Push Through: Spiritual/Mental/Physical Work That Will Be Done Today:

Nightly Thoughts

Time: I Feel:

Today's Accomplishment: Today I Had To Change:

I Believe: I Spent Time Learning:

Today's Challenges: I Connected With:

Today My Business Needed: I Sharpened My Skills/Products By:

Business Minded Daily

Date: Mood:

Morning Thoughts

Today's Affirmation: I Am Creating:

My Motivation: Today I Will Not Forget To:

I Will Push Through: Spiritual/Mental/Physical Work That Will
                                Be Done Today:

Nightly Thoughts

Time: I Feel:

Today's Accomplishment: Today I Had To Change:

I Believe: I Spent Time Learning:

Today's Challenges: I Connected With:

Today My Business Needed: I Sharpened My Skills/Products By:

Business Minded Daily

Date: Mood:

Morning Thoughts

Today's Affirmation: I Am Creating:

My Motivation: Today I Will Not Forget To:

I Will Push Through: Spiritual/Mental/Physical Work That Will
                                           Be Done Today:

Nightly Thoughts

Time: I Feel:

Today's Accomplishment: Today I Had To Change:

I Believe: I Spent Time Learning:

Today's Challenges: I Connected With:

Today My Business Needed: I Sharpened My Skills/Products By:

Business Minded Daily

Date: Mood:

Morning Thoughts

Today's Affirmation: I Am Creating:

My Motivation: Today I Will Not Forget To:

I Will Push Through: Spiritual/Mental/Physical Work That Will
                                         Be Done Today:

Nightly Thoughts

Time: I Feel:

Today's Accomplishment: Today I Had To Change:

I Believe: I Spent Time Learning:

Today's Challenges: I Connected With:

Today My Business Needed: I Sharpened My Skills/Products By:

My Business Notes

Business Minded Daily

Date: Mood:

Morning Thoughts

Today's Affirmation: I Am Creating:

My Motivation: Today I Will Not Forget To:

I Will Push Through: Spiritual/Mental/Physical Work That Will
                                         Be Done Today:

Nightly Thoughts

Time: I Feel:

Today's Accomplishment: Today I Had To Change:

I Believe: I Spent Time Learning:

Today's Challenges: I Connected With:

Today My Business Needed: I Sharpened My Skills/Products By:

Business Minded Daily

Date: Mood:

Morning Thoughts

Today's Affirmation: I Am Creating:

My Motivation: Today I Will Not Forget To:

I Will Push Through: Spiritual/Mental/Physical Work That Will
                                             Be Done Today:

Nightly Thoughts

Time: I Feel:

Today's Accomplishment: Today I Had To Change:

I Believe: I Spent Time Learning:

Today's Challenges: I Connected With:

Today My Business Needed: I Sharpened My Skills/Products By:

I Thank God For The Vision.

Business Minded Daily

Date: Mood:

Morning Thoughts

Today's Affirmation: I Am Creating:

My Motivation: Today I Will Not Forget To:

I Will Push Through: Spiritual/Mental/Physical Work That Will
                                        Be Done Today:

Nightly Thoughts

Time: I Feel:

Today's Accomplishment: Today I Had To Change:

I Believe: I Spent Time Learning:

Today's Challenges: I Connected With:

Today My Business Needed: I Sharpened My Skills/Products By:

Business Minded Daily

Date: Mood:

Morning Thoughts

Today's Affirmation: I Am Creating:

My Motivation: Today I Will Not Forget To:

I Will Push Through: Spiritual/Mental/Physical Work That Will
                                         Be Done Today:

Nightly Thoughts

Time: I Feel:

Today's Accomplishment: Today I Had To Change:

I Believe: I Spent Time Learning:

Today's Challenges: I Connected With:

Today My Business Needed: I Sharpened My Skills/Products By:

My Business Notes

Business Minded Daily

Date: Mood:

Morning Thoughts

Today's Affirmation: I Am Creating:

My Motivation: Today I Will Not Forget To:

I Will Push Through: Spiritual/Mental/Physical Work That Will
                                         Be Done Today:

Nightly Thoughts

Time: I Feel:

Today's Accomplishment: Today I Had To Change:

I Believe: I Spent Time Learning:

Today's Challenges: I Connected With:

Today My Business Needed: I Sharpened My Skills/Products By:

Business Minded Daily

Date: Mood:

Morning Thoughts

Today's Affirmation: I Am Creating:

My Motivation: Today I Will Not Forget To:

I Will Push Through: Spiritual/Mental/Physical Work That Will
                                                  Be Done Today:

Nightly Thoughts

Time: I Feel:

Today's Accomplishment: Today I Had To Change:

I Believe: I Spent Time Learning:

Today's Challenges: I Connected With:

Today My Business Needed: I Sharpened My Skills/Products By:

My Business Notes

Business Minded Daily

Date: Mood:

Morning Thoughts

Today's Affirmation: I Am Creating:

My Motivation: Today I Will Not Forget To:

I Will Push Through: Spiritual/Mental/Physical Work That Will
                                               Be Done Today:

Nightly Thoughts

Time: I Feel:

Today's Accomplishment: Today I Had To Change:

I Believe: I Spent Time Learning:

Today's Challenges: I Connected With:

Today My Business Needed: I Sharpened My Skills/Products By:

Business Minded Daily

Date: Mood:

Morning Thoughts

Today's Affirmation: I Am Creating:

My Motivation: Today I Will Not Forget To:

I Will Push Through: Spiritual/Mental/Physical Work That Will
                                         Be Done Today:

Nightly Thoughts

Time: I Feel:

Today's Accomplishment: Today I Had To Change:

I Believe: I Spent Time Learning:

Today's Challenges: I Connected With:

Today My Business Needed: I Sharpened My Skills/Products By:

Business Minded Daily

Date: Mood:

Morning Thoughts

Today's Affirmation: I Am Creating:

My Motivation: Today I Will Not Forget To:

I Will Push Through: Spiritual/Mental/Physical Work That Will
                                         Be Done Today:

Nightly Thoughts

Time: I Feel:

Today's Accomplishment: Today I Had To Change:

I Believe: I Spent Time Learning:

Today's Challenges: I Connected With:

Today My Business Needed: I Sharpened My Skills/Products By:

276

My Business Notes

Business Minded Daily

Date: Mood:

Morning Thoughts

Today's Affirmation: I Am Creating:

My Motivation: Today I Will Not Forget To:

I Will Push Through: Spiritual/Mental/Physical Work That Will
                                               Be Done Today:

Nightly Thoughts

Time: I Feel:

Today's Accomplishment: Today I Had To Change:

I Believe: I Spent Time Learning:

Today's Challenges: I Connected With:

Today My Business Needed: I Sharpened My Skills/Products By:

278

Business Minded Daily

Date: Mood:

Morning Thoughts

Today's Affirmation: I Am Creating:

My Motivation: Today I Will Not Forget To:

I Will Push Through: Spiritual/Mental/Physical Work That Will
                                         Be Done Today:

Nightly Thoughts

Time: I Feel:

Today's Accomplishment: Today I Had To Change:

I Believe: I Spent Time Learning:

Today's Challenges: I Connected With:

Today My Business Needed: I Sharpened My Skills/Products By:

I Am Not Afraid To Learn From My Mistakes.

Business Minded Daily

Date: Mood:

Morning Thoughts

Today's Affirmation: I Am Creating:

My Motivation: Today I Will Not Forget To:

I Will Push Through: Spiritual/Mental/Physical Work That Will
                                         Be Done Today:

Nightly Thoughts

Time: I Feel:

Today's Accomplishment: Today I Had To Change:

I Believe: I Spent Time Learning:

Today's Challenges: I Connected With:

Today My Business Needed: I Sharpened My Skills/Products By:

Business Minded Daily

Date: Mood:

Morning Thoughts

Today's Affirmation: I Am Creating:

My Motivation: Today I Will Not Forget To:

I Will Push Through: Spiritual/Mental/Physical Work That Will
                                         Be Done Today:

Nightly Thoughts

Time: I Feel:

Today's Accomplishment: Today I Had To Change:

I Believe: I Spent Time Learning:

Today's Challenges: I Connected With:

Today My Business Needed: I Sharpened My Skills/Products By:

Business Minded Daily

Date: Mood:

Morning Thoughts

Today's Affirmation: I Am Creating:

My Motivation: Today I Will Not Forget To:

I Will Push Through: Spiritual/Mental/Physical Work That Will
                                                Be Done Today:

Nightly Thoughts

Time: I Feel:

Today's Accomplishment: Today I Had To Change:

I Believe: I Spent Time Learning:

Today's Challenges: I Connected With:

Today My Business Needed: I Sharpened My Skills/Products By:

Business Minded Daily

Date: Mood:

Morning Thoughts

Today's Affirmation: | I Am Creating:

My Motivation: | Today I Will Not Forget To:

I Will Push Through: | Spiritual/Mental/Physical Work That Will Be Done Today:

Nightly Thoughts

Time: | I Feel:

Today's Accomplishment: | Today I Had To Change:

I Believe: | I Spent Time Learning:

Today's Challenges: | I Connected With:

Today My Business Needed: | I Sharpened My Skills/Products By:

My Business Notes

Business Minded Daily

Date: Mood:

Morning Thoughts

Today's Affirmation: I Am Creating:

My Motivation: Today I Will Not Forget To:

I Will Push Through: Spiritual/Mental/Physical Work That Will
                                         Be Done Today:

Nightly Thoughts

Time: I Feel:

Today's Accomplishment: Today I Had To Change:

I Believe: I Spent Time Learning:

Today's Challenges: I Connected With:

Today My Business Needed: I Sharpened My Skills/Products By:

Business Minded Daily

Date: Mood:

Morning Thoughts

Today's Affirmation: I Am Creating:

My Motivation: Today I Will Not Forget To:

I Will Push Through: Spiritual/Mental/Physical Work That Will Be Done Today:

Nightly Thoughts

Time: I Feel:

Today's Accomplishment: Today I Had To Change:

I Believe: I Spent Time Learning:

Today's Challenges: I Connected With:

Today My Business Needed: I Sharpened My Skills/Products By:

My Business Is Not For Everyone.

Business Minded Daily

Date: Mood:

Morning Thoughts

Today's Affirmation: I Am Creating:

My Motivation: Today I Will Not Forget To:

I Will Push Through: Spiritual/Mental/Physical Work That Will
                                         Be Done Today:

Nightly Thoughts

Time: I Feel:

Today's Accomplishment: Today I Had To Change:

I Believe: I Spent Time Learning:

Today's Challenges: I Connected With:

Today My Business Needed: I Sharpened My Skills/Products By:

Business Minded Daily

Date: Mood:

Morning Thoughts

Today's Affirmation: I Am Creating:

My Motivation: Today I Will Not Forget To:

I Will Push Through: Spiritual/Mental/Physical Work That Will
                                         Be Done Today:

Nightly Thoughts

Time: I Feel:

Today's Accomplishment: Today I Had To Change:

I Believe: I Spent Time Learning:

Today's Challenges: I Connected With:

Today My Business Needed: I Sharpened My Skills/Products By:

My Business Notes

Business Minded Daily

Date: Mood:

Morning Thoughts

Today's Affirmation: I Am Creating:

My Motivation: Today I Will Not Forget To:

I Will Push Through: Spiritual/Mental/Physical Work That Will
                                         Be Done Today:

Nightly Thoughts

Time: I Feel:

Today's Accomplishment: Today I Had To Change:

I Believe: I Spent Time Learning:

Today's Challenges: I Connected With:

Today My Business Needed: I Sharpened My Skills/Products By:

Business Minded Daily

Date: Mood:

Morning Thoughts

Today's Affirmation: I Am Creating:

My Motivation: Today I Will Not Forget To:

I Will Push Through: Spiritual/Mental/Physical Work That Will
                                         Be Done Today:

Nightly Thoughts

Time: I Feel:

Today's Accomplishment: Today I Had To Change:

I Believe: I Spent Time Learning:

Today's Challenges: I Connected With:

Today My Business Needed: I Sharpened My Skills/Products By:

Business Minded Daily

Date: Mood:

Morning Thoughts

Today's Affirmation: I Am Creating:

My Motivation: Today I Will Not Forget To:

I Will Push Through: Spiritual/Mental/Physical Work That Will
                                         Be Done Today:

Nightly Thoughts

Time: I Feel:

Today's Accomplishment: Today I Had To Change:

I Believe: I Spent Time Learning:

Today's Challenges: I Connected With:

Today My Business Needed: I Sharpened My Skills/Products By:

294

I Believe In My Big Ideas.

Business Minded Daily

Date: Mood:

Morning Thoughts

Today's Affirmation: I Am Creating:

My Motivation: Today I Will Not Forget To:

I Will Push Through: Spiritual/Mental/Physical Work That Will Be Done Today:

Nightly Thoughts

Time: I Feel:

Today's Accomplishment: Today I Had To Change:

I Believe: I Spent Time Learning:

Today's Challenges: I Connected With:

Today My Business Needed: I Sharpened My Skills/Products By:

Business Minded Daily

Date: Mood:

Morning Thoughts

Today's Affirmation: I Am Creating:

My Motivation: Today I Will Not Forget To:

I Will Push Through: Spiritual/Mental/Physical Work That Will
                                       Be Done Today:

Nightly Thoughts

Time: I Feel:

Today's Accomplishment: Today I Had To Change:

I Believe: I Spent Time Learning:

Today's Challenges: I Connected With:

Today My Business Needed: I Sharpened My Skills/Products By:

297

Business Minded Daily

Date: Mood:

Morning Thoughts

Today's Affirmation: I Am Creating:

My Motivation: Today I Will Not Forget To:

I Will Push Through: Spiritual/Mental/Physical Work That Will
                                         Be Done Today:

Nightly Thoughts

Time: I Feel:

Today's Accomplishment: Today I Had To Change:

I Believe: I Spent Time Learning:

Today's Challenges: I Connected With:

Today My Business Needed: I Sharpened My Skills/Products By:

My Business Notes

Business Minded Daily

Date: Mood:

Morning Thoughts

Today's Affirmation: I Am Creating:

My Motivation: Today I Will Not Forget To:

I Will Push Through: Spiritual/Mental/Physical Work That Will
                                         Be Done Today:

Nightly Thoughts

Time: I Feel:

Today's Accomplishment: Today I Had To Change:

I Believe: I Spent Time Learning:

Today's Challenges: I Connected With:

Today My Business Needed: I Sharpened My Skills/Products By:

300

Business Minded Daily

Date: Mood:

Morning Thoughts

Today's Affirmation: I Am Creating:

My Motivation: Today I Will Not Forget To:

I Will Push Through: Spiritual/Mental/Physical Work That Will
                                         Be Done Today:

Nightly Thoughts

Time: I Feel:

Today's Accomplishment: Today I Had To Change:

I Believe: I Spent Time Learning:

Today's Challenges: I Connected With:

Today My Business Needed: I Sharpened My Skills/Products By:

My Ideas Are Doable.

Business Minded Daily

Date: Mood:

Morning Thoughts

Today's Affirmation:

My Motivation:

I Will Push Through:

I Am Creating:

Today I Will Not Forget To:

Spiritual/Mental/Physical Work That Will Be Done Today:

Nightly Thoughts

Time:

Today's Accomplishment:

I Believe:

Today's Challenges:

Today My Business Needed:

I Feel:

Today I Had To Change:

I Spent Time Learning:

I Connected With:

I Sharpened My Skills/Products By:

Business Minded Daily

Date: Mood:

Morning Thoughts

Today's Affirmation: I Am Creating:

My Motivation: Today I Will Not Forget To:

I Will Push Through: Spiritual/Mental/Physical Work That Will
                                         Be Done Today:

Nightly Thoughts

Time: I Feel:

Today's Accomplishment: Today I Had To Change:

I Believe: I Spent Time Learning:

Today's Challenges: I Connected With:

Today My Business Needed: I Sharpened My Skills/Products By:

Business Minded Daily

Date: Mood:

Morning Thoughts

Today's Affirmation: I Am Creating:

My Motivation: Today I Will Not Forget To:

I Will Push Through: Spiritual/Mental/Physical Work That Will
                                         Be Done Today:

Nightly Thoughts

Time: I Feel:

Today's Accomplishment: Today I Had To Change:

I Believe: I Spent Time Learning:

Today's Challenges: I Connected With:

Today My Business Needed: I Sharpened My Skills/Products By:

My Business Notes

Business Minded Daily

Date: Mood:

Morning Thoughts

Today's Affirmation: I Am Creating:

My Motivation: Today I Will Not Forget To:

I Will Push Through: Spiritual/Mental/Physical Work That Will
                                         Be Done Today:

Nightly Thoughts

Time: I Feel:

Today's Accomplishment: Today I Had To Change:

I Believe: I Spent Time Learning:

Today's Challenges: I Connected With:

Today My Business Needed: I Sharpened My Skills/Products By:

I Believe In What I Am Doing.

Business Minded Daily

Date: Mood:

Morning Thoughts

Today's Affirmation: I Am Creating:

My Motivation: Today I Will Not Forget To:

I Will Push Through: Spiritual/Mental/Physical Work That Will
                                             Be Done Today:

Nightly Thoughts

Time: I Feel:

Today's Accomplishment: Today I Had To Change:

I Believe: I Spent Time Learning:

Today's Challenges: I Connected With:

Today My Business Needed: I Sharpened My Skills/Products By:

Business Minded Daily

Date: Mood:

Morning Thoughts

Today's Affirmation: I Am Creating:

My Motivation: Today I Will Not Forget To:

I Will Push Through: Spiritual/Mental/Physical Work That Will
                                         Be Done Today:

Nightly Thoughts

Time: I Feel:

Today's Accomplishment: Today I Had To Change:

I Believe: I Spent Time Learning:

Today's Challenges: I Connected With:

Today My Business Needed: I Sharpened My Skills/Products By:

Business Minded Daily

Date: Mood:

Morning Thoughts

Today's Affirmation: I Am Creating:

My Motivation: Today I Will Not Forget To:

I Will Push Through: Spiritual/Mental/Physical Work That Will
                                               Be Done Today:

Nightly Thoughts

Time: I Feel:

Today's Accomplishment: Today I Had To Change:

I Believe: I Spent Time Learning:

Today's Challenges: I Connected With:

Today My Business Needed: I Sharpened My Skills/Products By:

Business Minded Daily

Date: Mood:

Morning Thoughts

Today's Affirmation: I Am Creating:

My Motivation: Today I Will Not Forget To:

I Will Push Through: Spiritual/Mental/Physical Work That Will
                                               Be Done Today:

Nightly Thoughts

Time: I Feel:

Today's Accomplishment: Today I Had To Change:

I Believe: I Spent Time Learning:

Today's Challenges: I Connected With:

Today My Business Needed: I Sharpened My Skills/Products By:

I Am Only Getting Better.

Business Minded Daily

Date: Mood:

Morning Thoughts

Today's Affirmation: I Am Creating:

My Motivation: Today I Will Not Forget To:

I Will Push Through: Spiritual/Mental/Physical Work That Will
                                         Be Done Today:

Nightly Thoughts

Time: I Feel:

Today's Accomplishment: Today I Had To Change:

I Believe: I Spent Time Learning:

Today's Challenges: I Connected With:

Today My Business Needed: I Sharpened My Skills/Products By:

Business Minded Daily

Date: Mood:

Morning Thoughts

Today's Affirmation: I Am Creating:

My Motivation: Today I Will Not Forget To:

I Will Push Through: Spiritual/Mental/Physical Work That Will Be Done Today:

Nightly Thoughts

Time: I Feel:

Today's Accomplishment: Today I Had To Change:

I Believe: I Spent Time Learning:

Today's Challenges: I Connected With:

Today My Business Needed: I Sharpened My Skills/Products By:

Business Minded Daily

Date: Mood:

Morning Thoughts

Today's Affirmation: I Am Creating:

My Motivation: Today I Will Not Forget To:

I Will Push Through: Spiritual/Mental/Physical Work That Will
                                         Be Done Today:

Nightly Thoughts

Time: I Feel:

Today's Accomplishment: Today I Had To Change:

I Believe: I Spent Time Learning:

Today's Challenges: I Connected With:

Today My Business Needed: I Sharpened My Skills/Products By:

Business Minded Daily

Date: Mood:

Morning Thoughts

Today's Affirmation: I Am Creating:

My Motivation: Today I Will Not Forget To:

I Will Push Through: Spiritual/Mental/Physical Work That Will
                                         Be Done Today:

Nightly Thoughts

Time: I Feel:

Today's Accomplishment: Today I Had To Change:

I Believe: I Spent Time Learning:

Today's Challenges: I Connected With:

Today My Business Needed: I Sharpened My Skills/Products By:

Business Minded Daily

Date: Mood:

Morning Thoughts

Today's Affirmation: I Am Creating:

My Motivation: Today I Will Not Forget To:

I Will Push Through: Spiritual/Mental/Physical Work That Will
                                         Be Done Today:

Nightly Thoughts

Time: I Feel:

Today's Accomplishment: Today I Had To Change:

I Believe: I Spent Time Learning:

Today's Challenges: I Connected With:

Today My Business Needed: I Sharpened My Skills/Products By:

318

Business Minded Daily

Date: Mood:

Morning Thoughts

Today's Affirmation: I Am Creating:

My Motivation: Today I Will Not Forget To:

I Will Push Through: Spiritual/Mental/Physical Work That Will
                                         Be Done Today:

Nightly Thoughts

Time: I Feel:

Today's Accomplishment: Today I Had To Change:

I Believe: I Spent Time Learning:

Today's Challenges: I Connected With:

Today My Business Needed: I Sharpened My Skills/Products By:

Everyday Is A Profitable Day.

Made in the USA
San Bernardino, CA
19 February 2020